Too Smart for This

Too Smart for This

A Journal to Build Self-Trust
and Stop Settling for Less
Than You Deserve

ALEXIS BARBER

A TarcherPerigee Book

an imprint of Penguin Random House LLC
1745 Broadway, New York, NY 10019
penguinrandomhouse.com

Book design by Shannon Nicole Plunkett

Trade paperback ISBN: 9780593850800
Ebook ISBN: 9780593855119
Library of Congress Control Number: 2024937727

Printed in the United States of America
1st Printing

The authorized representative in the EU for product safety and compliance is
Penguin Random House Ireland, Morrison Chambers, 32 Nassau Street,
Dublin D02 YH68, Ireland, https://eu-contact.penguin.ie.

To all the girlfriends whose light helped me see my own

Contents

Introduction

At a brunch spot in New York City, I sat down excited to kiki with two of my best friends after a long and exhausting week. We had finally found time in our busy schedules to meet, and we were all looking forward to sharing the latest updates on our lives over Aperol spritzes.

My first friend briefly mumbled something about being nominated for an award in her industry and landing a huge freelance client—before jumping into a detailed update about an ex-fling of hers liking her Instagram story at around 11:30 p.m. on Thursday, which had completely consumed her mind for the past few days. Had he responded to her texts from months ago or broken up with his girlfriend? No, but he had kept her on a string ever since they'd ended things.

My second friend glossed over her recent accomplishments—running a half-marathon and being promoted early at a competitive firm—to talk at length about a friend who had been crossing her boundaries and making her feel terrible since they were teenagers. Yet another snide comment from this friend had sent her into an anxious spiral that had lasted most of the past week.

After her rant concluded, it was my turn. I failed to mention the great progress I was making in my complicated family relationships and my own exciting career opportunities, instead discussing my new diet and a wellness trend I was obsessing over, while describing my physical appearance with disdain.

I'm sure you've been here before. You can't believe your amazing, intelligent, accomplished friend is still worrying about the stupid man who's not good enough for her, the bad friend she's hanging on to out of guilt, or the fitness trend that's hiding the fact that she doesn't feel worthy enough inside. You just want to shake her and say, "You're too smart for this BS! Too beautiful! Too kind!" I caught my friends doing it this time: whenever one of us spoke about these trivial situations we were dealing with, the others at the table would lock eyes and ask in a loving but concerned tone why that person was spending time caring about something that was so beneath the essence of who we all were.

It pained me to watch my inspiring crew of ambitious friends accept anything less than what I knew they deserved, and I realized that my own battles were keeping me from doing that for myself. The hours I wasted thinking about my food or how to dress in a flattering way could've been spent having fun or learning something new. Imagine how much better off we would all be if we were using our precious brain space on things that made us happy.

That's where this journal comes in. If you're sick of the nagging feeling that you're not enough, no matter what you do or how much you accomplish, the prompts ahead will help you accept who you are, come up with a clear vision for your future, and manage the weight of society's expectations while building a life on your own terms. They're designed to create a foundation of self-love and self-trust that will let you stay aligned with your values as you move toward your aspirations with confidence instead of letting insecurities hold you back.

The journal is divided into four sections, one for every quarter of the year, each with a different focus: reflecting on lessons from your past, cultivating your vision for the future, defining values and rules that work for you, and dealing with struggles or roadblocks. Each section contains weekly deep dives on a theme within that focus, with a contemplative reset at the end of every quarter.

If you fill out the journal week by week as intended, you'll spend a year bringing your inner strength and wisdom out into the light of your life—but it's important to note that there's no wrong way to use this journal. If you feel energized to do a few weeks in one go, you can. If you miss a week, don't feel guilty; just jump back in when you're able. If you benefit from a steady routine, schedule some journaling time every Saturday morning over a cup of your favorite tea. If you prefer to journal a few times a week, whenever the mood strikes, go for it. The point is: it's your journal, and you should feel free to use it in the way that's most helpful for you.

And I hope that it is very helpful. By the time you're done with this journal, I hope you have let go of habits that aren't serving you and embraced your intelligent, capable, hardworking self so you can reach your full potential. I know you can do it—you're too smart not to.

Happy journaling,

Alexis Barber

Q1

How Did You Get Here?

started cognitive behavioral therapy at age twenty. The ambitious go-getter in me was irritated when my therapist kept driving the sessions toward questions about my childhood. Couldn't she help me focus on my problems *today*, like getting the best internship, navigating the dynamics in my sorority house, and passing French class? Why did she need to know about my relationship with my mother?

But it turns out she was right. Almost all the ways we act and react today are rooted in something we experienced as a child. Unfortunately for those of us who are deeply impatient, this means that if you *really* want to get better, enjoy your life, and develop healthy coping mechanisms, you have to take a look at all those seemingly tiny turning points in childhood that eventually led to adult you apologizing for everything you think, say, or do, or keeping the same Subway order that you had at age seven.

I know, I hate this too. I'm the type who wants a blueprint for improving my life that I can implement tomorrow—and if I could give you that, I absolutely would. But after years of working on my healing, I continue to discover that so many of the things that trigger me or influence my unhealthy habits are so painful because of the way young Alexis felt (sorority dynamics included). When you recognize why you're reacting to something, you can approach that narrative from a new angle so you can start going through your life with more authenticity and joy.

With some things, it's easy: you can just try a new Subway order! But with the big things—the ones that make you scared to trust new romantic partners or look at your body in the mirror—there's going to be some tears. There might be some heartbreak on behalf of littler you, and afterward, some heartbreak for how long you lived with that pain. But what's on the other side of that heartbreak is so much better.

When I reluctantly reflected on my own childhood in therapy, I recognized that most of my life choices had been oriented toward being liked by others. I learned that this was my survival mechanism as a child. Growing up poor meant that people were often looking down on me, and I felt I needed to excel in academic and social environments to get out of my low-income community and reach some form of stability. While this helped me become successful at a young age, it also led me to feel ultra-triggered when people didn't respect or like me even though I was now financially stable. That core need to be impressive to everyone was helpful at one point, but it had become a totally unrealistic hindrance to my growth now.

Your formative struggles and their associated coping mechanisms may be different from mine, but they affect you just as deeply. That's how life works. We have to start our healing by looking backward so that we can then look forward with more clarity.

If you're achievement-oriented like me, think of this portion of the journal as the research-and-outlining stage of a paper or project: you're assessing the current landscape and deciding how to approach the challenge at hand with the right context. You're a smart person, and I know you know that you must do the right preparation to get the best outcome. When you avoid reflecting on the past in the name of getting to the next step, it's like producing a research paper without any research; the paper will be messy and built on nothing of substance.

So I urge you to focus on reflection with the same excitement you'd use to focus on a fresh new plan. Some of these prompts may be heavy, but they have a purpose—and if they're too much, know you can always come back to them later. Get excited: you're starting on a journey that will help you grow!

Week 1

WHY WE ARE WHO WE ARE

Have you ever met someone who has such a strong sense of self that it makes you immediately respect them? Maybe they have a distinct style, personality, or career path, and they're so unapologetic about it that it makes you wonder about your own sense of self. We can only become unshakably confident when we know who we are and why, and the best way to do that is to start questioning why you do what you do.

When you first meet someone, how do you describe yourself? What parts of that identity are most important to you?

_____

_____

_____

_____

_____

_____

_____

_____

What single characteristic in your self-description has most influenced your life today? Why?

_____

_____

_____

_____

_____

_____

_____

_____

_____

Over the course of your life, who influenced you the most in the following areas and why? These can be family members or fictional characters you loved as a child (candidly, many ambitious women I encounter reference Blair Waldorf).

In school: _____

_____

_____

In relationships: _____

_____

_____

In health: _____

_____

_____

In friendships: _____

_____

_____

In money: _____

_____

_____

Week 2

CHILDHOOD LIMITING BELIEFS

A "limiting belief" is something you take as truth that influences how you act in the world. For example, believing that you "aren't good enough" to succeed in your job or "aren't good with money" may keep you from pursuing your dream career or becoming financially free. We can often find the root of limiting beliefs in what we were taught was fundamentally true as children—which often turns out not to be true at all.

How did your family talk about the following topics?
Do you have similar or differing opinions on any of them now?

Love: _____

_____

_____

Money: _____

_____

_____

Sex: _____

_____

_____

Jobs and education: _____

_____

_____

Politics: _____

_____

_____

Culture and race: _____

_____

_____

What would you say is your biggest limiting belief? When did you last notice that you were feeling constrained by it?

_____

_____

_____

_____

_____

_____

Identify your three most pressing limiting beliefs. For each one, craft a statement that competes with it that you can repeat to yourself when you notice the belief coming up for you.

Limiting belief: _____

_____

Competing statement: _____

_____

Limiting belief: _____

_____

Competing statement: _____

_____

Limiting belief: _____

_____

Competing statement: _____

_____

Week 3

MAKING SENSE OF OUR FAMILIES

A very simple truth that took me a long time to learn is that no one has a perfect family! I used to feel like I was the only one struggling with family issues, but as I've gotten older, I've realized nearly everyone has confusing and challenging family dynamics at times. So whether you lived in a two-parent home or in a home without any blood relatives, it's important to reflect on the dynamics that shaped you.

How did your parents or primary caregivers interact with each other? With your siblings and with you?

_____

_____

_____

_____

_____

_____

_____

_____

How did your siblings interact with each other and with you?

_____

_____

_____

_____

_____

_____

_____

_____

_____

How did your family members show or express love in your
household?

_____

_____

_____

_____

_____

_____

_____

_____

_____

_____

How do your family dynamics influence the way you run
your life today? (For example, are you constantly on call for
younger siblings, taking care of an elder, or paying for your
family's needs?)

_____

_____

_____

_____

_____

_____

_____

_____

_____

Week 4

FAMILY REFLECTIONS

Acknowledging our family norms and interactions is the first step toward growth, but it's also important to dig into the dynamics, unspoken rules, and communication styles that may affect how you show up in your family and in your other relationships. Identifying these themes can help you move out of unhealthy cycles and appreciate your family for who they are.

Reflect on a recent challenging family situation. It doesn't have to be super traumatic—any minor conflict will do. What emotions did it bring up for you? How did you cope with those emotions at the time, and how do you feel about it now? Write about any insights or lessons you've gained from that experience.

_____

_____

_____

_____

_____

_____

_____

_____

_____

_____

_____

_____

_____

Consider the role you play within your family dynamics.
(You may play different roles with different family members at
different times.) Are you a peacemaker, mediator, caregiver, or
something else? How does this role affect your relationships
with family members, and do you feel it's a role you want to
continue playing?

_____

_____

_____

_____

_____

_____

_____

_____

Write about your communication patterns within your family. Are there recurring conflicts or misunderstandings that arise? What could be contributing to these patterns?

_____

_____

_____

_____

_____

_____

_____

_____

_____

_____

_____

_____

_____

_____

Week 5

SELF-ESTEEM REFLECTIONS

Sometimes, until we consciously acknowledge it, the self-critical voice in our heads is the default for how we speak to ourselves. This can create cycles of negative self-esteem that keep us feeling stuck. If you're your own worst critic (most of us are!), this is the first step to changing the way you talk to yourself and opening the door to authentic self-love.

When did you first start talking negatively about yourself? What or who influenced you to do so? (There may be multiple influences.)

_____

_____

_____

_____

_____

_____

_____

_____

_____

_____

_____

_____

_____

What external factors have influenced your self-esteem? Are there things you feel like you "have" to do or be to feel worthy? Why do you think so?

_____

_____

_____

_____

_____

_____

_____

_____

_____

_____

_____

_____

_____

What are your five best qualities? How often do you tell yourself you're proud of these things?

_____

_____

_____

_____

_____

_____

_____

_____

_____

_____

_____

Week 6

RELATIONSHIP REFLECTIONS

Romantic relationships are a huge part of our lives, and they reveal a lot about how we feel about ourselves. Healthy relationships can be so fulfilling and supportive, and unhealthy ones can cause us lots of unnecessary pain. Identifying your beliefs here can help you get clear on your relationship to romantic love.

Where did you learn what a romantic relationship looks like? Consider your parents, other family members, and media portrayals. What healthy or unhealthy patterns do you notice?

_____

_____

_____

_____

_____

_____

_____

_____

_____

_____

_____

_____

_____

_____

When was your first romantic relationship or crush? What did you learn from it?

_____

_____

_____

_____

_____

_____

_____

_____

_____

What do you believe a healthy relationship looks like? Have you seen examples of that in your own family or life, or does this perception come from the media or your peers?

_____

_____

_____

_____

_____

_____

_____

_____

_____

_____

_____

_____

_____

Week 7

CAREER REFLECTIONS

Our upbringings have a huge impact on what careers we believe are possible for us. Maybe you wanted to be a doctor but a family member shot that idea down because you were a woman. Or maybe you wanted to be an artist but you felt too responsible for your family's financial situation to take such a risky career path. Getting clear on your real career interests will help you unlock more potential career fulfillment.

When you were little, what did you want to be when you grew up? Is your job at all similar to that now? Why or why not?

_____

_____

_____

_____

_____

_____

_____

Who did you look up to career-wise when you were growing up? (They can be real or fictional.) What do you think drew you to their careers?

_____

_____

_____

_____

_____

_____

_____

_____

_____

_____

_____

_____

_____

What are the cultural beliefs about careers that you grew up with? How did these change or impact what you believed to be true about your career options?

_____

_____

_____

_____

_____

_____

_____

_____

_____

_____

_____

_____

Week 8

FRIENDSHIP REFLECTIONS

Community is everything: when we feel connected to people, we feel love. Like all relationships, friendships can teach us a lot about ourselves. How do your friends change or influence your beliefs about yourself, and most importantly, how do they make you feel? Let's analyze the roots of your relationship to friendship.

Who were your first friends outside of your family? How did they make you feel?

_____

_____

_____

_____

_____

_____

_____

_____

_____

_____

Do you think you're a good friend? Who or what most influenced what that looks like to you?

_____

_____

_____

_____

_____

_____

_____

_____

_____

_____

_____

_____

_____

_____

What does a good friendship look like to you? What about a bad one? Where did you learn this?

_____

_____

_____

_____

_____

_____

_____

_____

_____

_____

_____

_____

_____

_____

_____

Week 9

MONEY REFLECTIONS

Money is crucial to our survival, and it can also feel super complicated. Our beliefs about money can cause lots of anxiety, but when we face our discomfort head-on, it can become way less scary than you might think. Let's take control of our narratives about money by getting to the bottom of where and why they originated.

What are the top two or three things your family taught you about money?

_____

_____

_____

_____

_____

_____

_____

_____

How did money impact your feeling of safety growing up?

_____

_____

_____

_____

_____

_____

_____

_____

Think about how you treat money today. Where do you think
you got that example?

_____

_____

_____

_____

_____

_____

_____

_____

_____

_____

Write about your ideal relationship with money. How do you get there? What affirmation might help you feel more comfortable with money?

_____

_____

_____

_____

_____

_____

_____

_____

_____

Week 10

CHILDHOOD FEARS

I consider myself a moderately anxious person now (my heart rate is definitely constantly fluctuating due to life's curveballs), but I was *incredibly* anxious as a child. When I reflect on what I've overcome since I was little, I realize that I have so much more power than I knew at the time. Many of our childhood fears are rational, but many don't serve us as adults, and when we look closer at them, we realize we're holding on to them out of habit rather than necessity. Let's put some of these to bed.

What were some things you were afraid of when you were a child? When did those fears start to dissipate? Are any of them still a part of your life?

_____

_____

_____

_____

_____

_____

_____

_____

What is one fear from your childhood that you've been able to overcome? What is one that still lives in you?

_____

_____

_____

_____

_____

_____

_____

_____

How would your life look different if you overcame more of your fears? How can you use the fears you have overcome in the past as reminders that you can face things in the future?

_____

_____

_____

Week 11

TRANSFORMING SHAME INTO OUR SUPERPOWER

Often when we're questioning why we do or don't accept something about ourselves, we can trace it back to our relationship with shame. Shame often keeps us from being our authentic selves, and when we question our relationship with it, we get closer to our own sense of confidence.

What is one thing in your life you're ashamed of? Pause—take a deep breath and remind yourself everyone has things they're ashamed of. What societal or cultural influences may have contributed to these feelings? How has shame manifested in your thoughts, emotions, and behaviors?

_____

_____

_____

_____

_____

_____

_____

_____

_____

_____

_____

_____

_____

_____

When do you judge yourself the most? Why do you do so?

_____

_____

_____

_____

_____

_____

_____

_____

We can transform our shame into strength by understanding its roots and changing it into a positive thing about ourselves. What actions or mindset shifts might you take to achieve this transformation? Create an affirmation that you can use next time you're feeling guilt or shame.

_____

_____

_____

_____

_____

_____

_____

_____

_____

_____

_____

_____

Week 12

STAYING TRUE TO YOURSELF WHILE EVOLVING

Before we move on to the next quarter, it's time to look at how you've evolved as a person over the past few weeks. You've likely learned a lot about yourself and may be feeling many feelings for your younger self. Use these prompts to remember what you loved about younger you so you can take it with you as we embark on the rest of this journey!

What is something you did as a child that brought you joy that you can integrate into your lifestyle now? How will you do this?

_____

_____

_____

_____

_____

_____

_____

_____

What values were present in your childhood that you want to take with you into the future?

_____

_____

_____

_____

_____

_____

_____

_____

Write a letter to your younger self. Tell them how you've gotten to where you are now. What would make them proud? What would make them feel safe?

_____

_____

_____

Week 13

QUARTERLY RESET
Q1

Can you believe you've already been journaling for three months? Congratulations on making it this far! Let's take this as an opportunity to pause and look back at all the work you've done reflecting on your past, before gearing up for next quarter's theme: finding your vision.

Over the past three months, what were your significant achievements, and in what areas did you see the most growth? Pay attention to the areas of life we touched on: family, personal life, professional life, relationships, money, and friendships.

_____

_____

_____

_____

_____

_____

_____

_____

Reflect on your self-care practices over the past quarter. How have these practices supported your physical, mental, and emotional well-being?

_____

_____

_____

_____

_____

_____

_____

_____

_____

_____

_____

_____

_____

Consider moments when you felt the most stressed or unbalanced. What triggered these feelings, and how did you respond? Identify patterns or recurring themes in your stressors.

_____

_____

_____

_____

_____

_____

_____

_____

_____

_____

_____

_____

Think back to where you were when you started this quarter.
What was that person struggling with, and how have you
addressed it? What are you struggling with now, and how do
you want to approach that in the next phase of your
self-growth?

_____

_____

_____

_____

_____

_____

_____

_____

_____

_____

_____

Finding Your Vision

Daydreaming is a superpower. It's something we all do—living in fictional worlds is often easier than facing our realities. From the ages of four to fifteen, I was likely to be found with my nose buried in a book, devouring the universes created by authors of young adult novels rather than looking up at the chaotic house I lived in with my seven younger siblings. Often we get so used to distracting ourselves with our dreams that we don't remember we're also in charge of our realities. Sometimes the only thing between you and what you want is whether you believe you can have it.

But, whew, society certainly hasn't made it easy for us to think we can have what we want. Stereotypes infiltrate our self-esteem from childhood. This is especially true for women: we're not good at math, we should be thinner, we shouldn't be too loud, we should be nicer. We are only rewarded when we're "humble." When a woman "makes it," her merit is questioned, and people—including other women who can't fathom someone existing outside the boxes they've squeezed themselves into—villainize her for her happiness. It's no wonder we don't believe we can realize our dreams in full color: *we haven't been allowed to.*

On one hand, our dreams are our own. No one has the same dream as you, the same path as you, or the same destiny as you. We're raised to conceive of others, especially other women, as competition, but when you think about it, no one wants *exactly* what you want, which is why it's useless to compare yourself to anyone but yourself.

At the same time, our dreams are what connect us. Your dreams are not just for you. In 2022, I interviewed Olamide Olowe, founder of the skincare company Topicals, on my podcast *Too Smart for This.* Something she said stuck with me (and the hundreds of thousands of people who viewed the clip online): "You really do need to live in your purpose and in your gift, because someone else's destiny is actually tied to you becoming who you are. If you weren't you, there's someone else two, three, five, ten years down the line who can't become who they need to become. I think about all the women I've looked up to, all the people I've looked up to, and had it not been for this person or that person, I just would not be who I'm supposed to be. So on days when you feel like you can't do it or you're tired, rest, but also know that it's not for you. . . . Someone else's whole destiny is tied to you being who you are."

When you deny yourself what you want, you deny everyone who comes after you that gift as well. So as you embark on this section of the journal, I beg you not to hold back on deciding what you want. Women have settled for so long. We've bitten our tongues, run the world from the sidelines, and ignored our aspirations to protect our safety. We've contorted ourselves into perfect beings, only to be undermined and destroyed for that same perfection. If you're lucky enough today to have an ounce of ambition, a snippet of what you want for yourself, it's not only your destiny to go after it— it's what's best for the entire world and everyone coming after you.

Week 14

IDENTIFYING JOY

Collectively, we don't have enough joy in our lives. In a world constrained by criticism, we're often operating to avoid disappointing people instead of for our own happiness. If you start this section without considering what makes **you** genuinely smile, you will create goals using the framework of a society that doesn't have your best interest at heart. Identifying the things that bring you joy should be your anchor as you identify your true dreams.

When was the last time you felt pure, unadulterated joy? A belly laugh that almost made you cry, a deep sense of appreciation while you walked through your favorite neighborhood, or a sense of true accomplishment after building something you loved?

_____

_____

_____

_____

_____

_____

_____

In which areas of your life do you feel the most joy? Family relationships, romantic relationships, friendships, career, hobbies?

_____

_____

_____

_____

_____

_____

_____

_____

What would intentionally adding more joy to your life look like?

_____

_____

_____

_____

_____

_____

_____

_____

_____

This week, make it a point to note the joy you're feeling on a daily basis. When were the moments that made you smile without thinking about it? Keep a list and come back to it when you need guidance.

_____

_____

_____

_____

_____

_____

_____

_____

_____

Week 15

LIKES VS. LOVES

So many of us are used to settling for less than we're worth. (See: your best friend dating that mediocre guy who isn't terrible but isn't amazing to her either.) Conflating things that we merely like with things that we truly love is a recipe for disappointment down the line. This week, think about what really makes you sparkle as opposed to what's just enough to keep you satisfied.

Looking back on your life, are there moments when you settled for things you liked rather than loved in a relationship, job, or other area? What made you do that?

_____

_____

_____

_____

_____

_____

_____

_____

_____

What is blocking you from only allowing the things you love
into your life?

_____

_____

_____

_____

_____

_____

_____

_____

Take an inventory of your past and make a list of at least one
thing you settled for in each of the following areas of life.
Compare that to what you loved (or believe you would've loved)
in those situations.

Career: _____

_____

_____

Love: _____

_____

_____

Friendships: _____

_____

_____

Family: _____

_____

_____

Money: _____

_____

_____

Health: _____

_____

_____

Week 16

MAGIC IN THE MUNDANE

We often wait for important milestones (hello, promotion!) to celebrate. Yet inevitably, when those moments come around, they never feel quite as good as we imagined they would. When focusing on our big dreams, we have to remember that accomplishing them won't always fulfill us—what's truly fulfilling is the fact that we believed in ourselves enough to show up for that dream every day. And while we're living in that everyday, it's important to find magic in our mundane.

Think about your day so far. What were the little things that went well and made you happy or proud? It could be your coffee order tasting just right, the sun coming out after a week of clouds, or making progress on a work project.

_____

_____

_____

_____

_____

_____

_____

_____

_____

_____

_____

Identify something you were successful at in the past. What days or moments were most joyful for you throughout that process?

_____

_____

_____

_____

_____

_____

_____

_____

_____

_____

How can you celebrate small, everyday moments like the ones you've described here as you move forward?

_____

_____

_____

_____

_____

_____

_____

_____

_____

_____

_____

_____

Week 17

DREAMING BIG

Now that we're grounded in our core wants, it's time to visualize our unlimited lives. Remember, your dreams are yours for a reason, so let's not hold back here!

List a few dreams you had when you were younger—anything from the pet you might have wanted to the city you wanted to live in. Dig deep and connect with the dreams of your younger self.

_____

_____

_____

_____

_____

_____

_____

_____

_____

What are some things you wanted so badly in the past that you now have?

_____

_____

_____

_____

_____

_____

_____

_____

What would you ask for if you knew the answer would be yes? Make a list of things you've desired, big and small, material and immaterial. This is a great prompt to think about after meditating or on a long walk—it should be fun!

_____

_____

_____

Week 18

DAYDREAMING

Health and Wellness

It's time to get specific. And we're starting off with the most important thing: your health and wellness. Ugh, I know. It can be so hard to prioritize this. But taking care of our bodies and minds is necessary for us to live purposeful lives, so we've got to face it head-on. And when we approach the subject from a foundation of self-acceptance, I promise it's not so bad!

What is your relationship like with your physical and mental health? When you've faced setbacks in the past, what has helped you get back on track?

_____

_____

_____

_____

_____

_____

_____

_____

_____

_____

_____

Are there health concerns you have, either physical or mental?
What would it look like to resolve those issues?

_____

_____

_____

_____

_____

_____

_____

_____

_____

_____

When you imagine the healthiest version of yourself, what does that look like to you? If you were to embody this version of yourself, what would you have to let go of to achieve it? What would you get to add to your life?

_____

_____

_____

_____

_____

_____

_____

_____

_____

_____

_____

_____

Week 19

DAYDREAMING

Relationships and Friendships

Connection is everything. The people we surround ourselves with can be sources of so much joy for us—and us for them. When it comes to relationships and friendships, it's important to feel safety and trust, so we must examine how we interact with others to make it happen. Building on the assessments you made in Q1, it's time to visualize your relationships in the most positive light possible.

What do happy, fulfilling friendships look like to you?

_____

_____

_____

_____

_____

_____

_____

_____

_____

What does a happy, fulfilling romantic relationship look like to you?

_____

_____

_____

_____

_____

_____

_____

_____

What does a happy, fulfilling relationship with your family look like to you? (This may be different for different family members!)

_____

_____

_____

_____

_____

_____

_____

_____

_____

Can you identify any of these positive relationship experiences in your current life? How can you cultivate more of them?

_____

_____

_____

_____

_____

_____

_____

_____

_____

_____

Week 20

DAYDREAMING

Career and Money

Careers can be incredibly fulfilling for us, but only if we're intentional about what we want. If we passively float along our career paths, we're likely to wake up one day and realize we're unsatisfied or even miserable in our jobs. It all starts with dreaming of what we want, so let's dream big here.

If money wasn't a concern, what would you do with your time? What would your career look like?

_____

_____

_____

_____

_____

_____

_____

_____

_____

_____

_____

_____

Write out what your dream day in your most fulfilling career would look like. Who do you work with? What do you get to do? Who do you get to serve?

_____

_____

_____

_____

_____

_____

_____

_____

_____

Financially, how much money would you want every month or year to feel abundant? What would you spend it on?

_____

_____

_____

_____

_____

_____

_____

_____

_____

_____

_____

_____

_____

Week 21

DAYDREAMING

Lifestyle

We've spent the past few weeks of this journal daydreaming. It's kinda fun, right? This week, let's synthesize everything we dreamed about and visualize our ideal life.

Write a list of everything you want, small or big, from the shoes you keep seeing on Instagram to the dream house in the countryside. This should be fun—keep writing until you can't think of anything else!

_____

_____

_____

_____

_____

_____

_____

_____

_____

Imagine what a perfect day would be like in your current reality—your current job, current home, current relationship, and so on. Write a journal entry describing that imaginary perfect day as if it has just happened.

_____

_____

_____

_____

_____

_____

_____

_____

_____

_____

_____

_____

Write the same journal entry about a perfect day as though it's five years from now. What has changed and what has stayed the same? What do you have now, and how do you feel?

_____

_____

_____

_____

_____

_____

_____

_____

_____

_____

_____

_____

_____

Week 22

VISION BOARDS AND VISUALIZING

Now that we've taken inventory of our daydreams, it's time to take a deep dive with vision boards. Whether or not you're a visual thinker, vision boards are a great way to stay motivated and inspired, and nowadays they're easier than ever to make online using apps like Pinterest or Canva. Make these vision boards digitally or physically, and revisit them often to remind yourself of your goals!

First, create a general vision board that has the big things you see for your life on it. These are things you want one day, but maybe not right now. (For example, maybe you want to be a CEO or move to London someday, but you're still several steps away.) Take a look at your big dreams from Week 17 to create this vision board, and find specific images online to represent them. Journal any thoughts and feelings that arise.

_____

_____

_____

_____

_____

_____

_____

_____

_____

_____

_____

_____

_____

Next, create a vision board for the next season of your life. This could be the quarter ahead or the year ahead, but it should be the not-too-distant future. Realistically, what do you want your daily life to look like? Get specific—if you're saving money, use an image of the exact amount you want to save, and if you're trying to drink more water, use an image of a water bottle. Journal any thoughts and feelings that arise.

_____

_____

_____

_____

_____

_____

Week 23

FINDING INSPIRATION

Listen, sometimes we get trapped in a funk that keeps us from feeling connected to our desires. Or sometimes we get so frustrated and discouraged that we think we'll never be able to get where we're trying to go. Use this week's prompts and ideas to reconnect with your inspiration.

What is something you thought you wanted but when you got it, you realized it didn't fulfill you? Why didn't it?

_____

_____

_____

_____

_____

_____

_____

_____

_____

_____

Conversely, what's something in your life that has unexpectedly brought you a lot of joy?

_____

_____

_____

_____

_____

_____

_____

_____

_____

When you look at media, the people around you, and your network of peers, who do you get the most inspiration from?

_____

_____

_____

Week 24

ENVY AND COMPARISON

Focusing on our goals is a good thing, but it can make it easier to fixate on others who already have what we're working toward. Then we can start feeling inadequate and jealous. Instead of getting destroyed by that feeling, we can return to our foundation of self-worth and remind ourselves that it's impossible to truly compare two people's unique situations—and that doing so does not help us get any closer to our dreams.

Think of a time in the past when you used to constantly compare yourself to someone. How and when did you stop doing that? What stopped the obsession?

_____

_____

_____

_____

_____

_____

_____

_____

Who are you most often comparing yourself to? Is it through social media or in real life? What about this person do you admire or are you bothered by?

_____

_____

_____

_____

_____

_____

_____

_____

_____

_____

_____

_____

_____

Who is someone who currently has what you want? Instead of letting them remind you of what you don't have, how can you let them expand your vision of what's possible for yourself?

_____

_____

_____

_____

_____

_____

_____

_____

_____

_____

_____

Week 25

GRATITUDE IS THE GOAT

On the journey to our big dreams, ambitious girlies like me tend to get impatient. The key to avoiding this feeling is gratitude. On days when you have big failures, the thing that will help you come back to yourself is simply gratitude for what you do have and who you already are.

When you look at your life now, do you have some of the things you wished for years ago? What are they? Express gratitude for them.

_____

_____

_____

_____

_____

_____

_____

_____

_____

What are some privileges you have that you don't recognize often enough? How do these help you live a better life?

_____

_____

_____

_____

_____

_____

_____

_____

_____

Think about your past self and everything that past you has been through. Think about yourself at your lowest point and write a letter to past you, thanking them for everything they did to help you get here.

_____

_____

Week 26

QUARTERLY RESET
Q2

You're halfway through the year and halfway through this journal—nice work! Before we move on to Q3, let's take a moment to pause and reflect on what you've learned about finding your vision over the past three months.

Over the past three months, what were your significant achievements, and in what areas did you see the most growth? Pay attention to all areas of life: family, personal life, professional life, relationships, money, and friendships.

_____

_____

_____

_____

_____

_____

_____

_____

Reflect on your self-care practices over the past quarter. How have these practices supported your physical, mental, and emotional well-being?

_____

_____

_____

_____

_____

_____

_____

_____

_____

_____

_____

_____

_____

_____

Consider moments when you felt the most stressed or
unbalanced. What triggered these feelings, and how did you
respond? Identify patterns or recurring themes in your stressors.

_____

_____

_____

_____

_____

_____

_____

_____

_____

_____

_____

_____

Think back to where you were when you started this quarter. What was that person struggling with, and how have you addressed it? What are you struggling with now, and how do you want to approach that in the next phase of your self-growth?

_____

_____

_____

_____

_____

_____

_____

_____

_____

_____

_____

_____

Q3

Your Personal Handbook

Name the most annoying, outdated meme on the internet. I'll go first: anything that has to do with "adulting." I shudder thinking about it . . . yet I'm guilty of contributing to anti-growing-up rhetoric. There's a unique pain that comes with being kicked off your parents' phone bill, dealing with worsening hangovers, and having to keep your composure in a work meeting with a micromanager boss in the name of "maturity." Ugh! But being an adult can also be *so* fun. You get to decorate your own place, buy your favorite snacks at the grocery store, and largely do whatever you want.

The problem with growing up is that it doesn't come with a handbook, so we have to create our own rules from scratch. And life is far too complex and individual for a one-size-fits-all guide. Instead, we must craft our own handbooks, our personalized sets of principles and frameworks for navigating the world according to our values.

I started creating frameworks for responding to life's curveballs when I found myself having a breakdown that required me to clear my calendar to cry every Tuesday or Wednesday afternoon. As I navigated overwhelm while managing my time in business school, I recognized that I needed a way to respond to these feelings that wouldn't impede my ability to function. I realized I needed different types of self-care at different moments, which I call the "Four Types of Rest," and when I inevitably faced burnout, I came up with other frameworks to help get me back on track. (We'll do a deep dive into these later in the quarter so you can create these rest protocols for yourself.)

Typically, it's painful moments that cause us to reassess what works for us and what doesn't, but in this part of the journal, you get to create your frameworks preemptively! Think of this as writing your own handbook for navigating your life. Instead of having to learn in the moment, future you can return to the reference point you've already created. Your frameworks will, of course, change as you go on, gather more information, and encounter new emotional challenges. But having something to fall back on when you're down will build your confidence and your sense of self. I offer some of my own frameworks in each prompt, but you don't have to follow them exactly because what works for one person may not necessarily be the right fit for another. If my frameworks are helpful for you, use them; if not, let them simply serve as inspiration for making your own. Let's do it!

Week 27

CHANGE YOUR EXPECTATIONS

I'm the first to encourage you to have high standards, but when we're working toward fundamental change in our lives, it's way easier to develop self-trust when we set our goals to be manageable rather than unattainable. Setting an unattainable goal is self-sabotage, because when you know you can't do something, you have an excuse to give up before you even try. Risking failure is scary, but taking manageable risks and succeeding is what lets you learn to trust yourself. So let's set *realistic* expectations here!

In the past, where have you put unrealistic expectations on yourself to succeed? What could've been different there?

_____

_____

_____

_____

_____

_____

_____

Take a look at some of the goals you set last quarter—for example, the vision board you made in Week 22. In the next six months, with all things considered, what are one or two things you can do each month to get you closer to your goals? Each week? Each day?

_____

_____

_____

_____

_____

Now break this into two categories: your minimum capacity each week (what you'll do if everything goes wrong and you barely have time to think) and your maximum capacity (what you'll do if everything goes right and you get it all done). For example: "I know I can cook at home at least two nights this week, even if I get a curveball thrown at me, but I also know I'd like to cook at home five nights this week if I could." What will you do each week if you're at minimum capacity? What about maximum capacity? Remember that even doing the minimum consistently will make a massive impact on your life!

_____

_____

_____

Week 28

ENJOYING THE PRESENT

Yesterday is gone. Tomorrow is unknown. As much as we love to plan out and visualize our lives, we will always, inevitably, be right here, right now. We miss out on our lives when we're obsessed with the future and when we stress over the past. Joy, happiness, and excitement can only really be felt when we are experiencing them *now*.

What's the last moment you remember being fully present in and having so much joy, fun, or laughter? What about that moment allowed you to feel present? Was it who you were with? Where you were? Something else?

_____

_____

_____

_____

_____

_____

_____

_____

_____

_____

_____

When do you feel the least connected to yourself and the least present? What are some ways you can minimize that going forward?

_____

_____

_____

_____

_____

_____

_____

_____

_____

A mantra I like to tell myself every day is "I'll never get this day back. What moments do I want to cherish?" What is your mantra for enjoying the present?

_____

_____

_____

_____

_____

_____

_____

_____

_____

_____

_____

_____

_____

Week 29

DESIGNING YOUR DAILY ROUTINES

Morning

Whoever said "The secret to your days is hidden in your morning routines" was one million percent correct. The best thing you can do for your mental health is starting your day on *your* terms, not anyone else's. My perfect formula (yours will be different!) is doing my skincare while listening to music or affirmations, going on a long walking meditation, and taking my supplements while I do my morning journaling. I don't check my phone until all of this is complete, to make sure that I'm not reacting to anything before I've centered myself with my goals, gratitude, and self-confidence practices.

Think about the best day you've had recently. What did your morning look like? Did it help set you up for success during the day? If so, how?

_____

_____

_____

_____

_____

_____

_____

_____

_____

_____

_____

_____

_____

_____

_____

Write out your ideal thirty-, sixty-, and ninety-minute morning routines. Keep a list of them so, based on the ebbs and flows of your life, you know what you can do to stay connected to yourself.

Thirty-minute routine: _____

_____

_____

_____

_____

Sixty-minute routine: _____

_____

_____

_____

_____

_____

Ninety-minute routine: _____

_____

_____

_____

_____

Week 30

DESIGNING YOUR DAILY ROUTINES

Evening

The morning routine is key, but it's nothing without the evening routine setting it up for success. The purpose of the evening routine is twofold: to prep for the next day and to genuinely wind down for quality sleep. This requires actually checking out of work—I like to make a to-do list for the next day, close out of email, and finish scrolling. If I have time, I'll go for a walk or work out, take an amazing shower, prep my hair for the next day, and then relax with *Housewives* or call my friends. Elite, huh?

What is your current evening routine? How do you feel in the morning? What causes you the most stress at night?

_____

_____

_____

_____

_____

_____

_____

_____

_____

_____

_____

_____

_____

_____

_____

Design your ideal thirty-, sixty-, and ninety-minute evening routines. Write these down and practice them based on the ebbs and flows of your life this week.

Thirty-minute routine: _____

_____

_____

_____

_____

_____

Sixty-minute routine: _____

_____

_____

_____

_____

_____

Ninety-minute routine: _____

_____

_____

_____

_____

_____

Week 31

THE FOUR TYPES OF REST

Blobbing

As I mentioned at the beginning of Q3, I use the framework of the Four Types of Rest to make sure I'm giving myself the kind of rest that I actually need. The first type is what I call "blobbing." We're constantly overstimulated today, and after a long week at work or a particularly tough day, sometimes all we need to do is lie on our couch, order our favorite takeout, and do nothing. This type of self-comfort may seem "lazy," but it's ultimately productive, because we're allowing ourselves to breathe before we return to working hard. A perfect blob day for me: take a long shower while listening to a funny podcast (nothing educational!), then do a face mask while I scroll mindlessly or catch up on reality TV. Usually, the next day I'm inspired to get back into my routines and take care of myself.

What is your perfect blob day? Go into as much detail as you want!

_____

_____

_____

_____

_____

_____

_____

_____

_____

What's something you _wouldn't_ include in a blob day, either
because it's too responsible (e.g., deep cleaning your home) or
because it may make you feel bad later (e.g., spending above
your means)?

_____

_____

_____

_____

_____

_____

_____

_____

_____

How can you give yourself permission to have a blob day
without guilt this week?

_____

_____

_____

_____

_____

_____

_____

_____

_____

Week 32

THE FOUR TYPES OF REST

Rejuvenation

Blobbing is great, but an equally necessary part of self-care is doing the things that are good for us, not just avoiding all of our responsibilities. This is what I call "rejuvenation": showing up for ourselves by doing the things that make our lives better and easier. When you're feeling scatterbrained or spread too thin, it's important to get back into your body (rather than your mind) and start to focus on what you can control. You can find comfort by going on a long walk, making plans that are in line with your goals, decluttering your apartment, or meal prepping for the week—anything that takes a moment out of the daily grind to set you up for success.

When you really feel like you've taken good care of yourself, what actions are you taking? Make a list of the things that you do to take care of your mind, body, soul, and living space.

_____

_____

_____

_____

_____

_____

_____

_____

_____

_____

_____

_____

_____

_____

_____

_____

When you're feeling out of control with your responsibilities,
what are three rejuvenating activities you can fall back on?
Practice at least one of them this week.

_____

_____

_____

Week 33

THE FOUR TYPES OF REST

Connection

The third type of rest in my framework is connection. We're nothing without our communities, and sometimes we self-isolate too much when we're trying to find comfort. Part of showing up for ourselves is relying on our communities for connection. When you're feeling uninspired, lonely, or overwhelmed, you can focus on connecting with others to get back to yourself. A few ways I like to do this are calling a family member, scheduling a monthly dinner with my friends, and using social media in a positive way (unfollowing accounts that don't add anything to my life and seeking out content that's more positive and aligned with my goals).

How do you currently connect best with others? In person, over the phone, through social media/texting? Which of these fills your cup the most and why?

_____

_____

_____

_____

_____

_____

_____

_____

_____

_____

_____

_____

_____

_____

_____

_____

_____

When you're feeling isolated, what are three connecting practices you can fall back on? Practice at least one of them this week.

_____

_____

_____

Week 34

THE FOUR TYPES OF REST

Pampering

The stereotypical version of self-care is what I like to call "pampering"—the fourth type of rest in my framework. Unlike blobbing, when you essentially do nothing, pampering is when you indulge in something special that makes you feel your best, like treating yourself to a massage or a facial. When you want to reward yourself for showing up for you, or maybe you're just feeling tired and need a boost, you can find comfort through a little pampering. My favorite way to add this into every week is with fun at-home baths and treating myself to nice things like candles.

Have you pampered yourself in the past? Are you someone who is afraid to pamper themselves or someone who might overindulge in it? Why do you think this is?

_____

_____

_____

_____

_____

_____

_____

_____

_____

_____

_____

_____

_____

_____

_____

_____

_____

Identify three types of pampering that you can integrate into your life: something small (like buying your favorite flowers), something medium (like taking a pottery class or getting a massage), and something big (like a vacation or staycation). Plan one of each of these into your next quarter!

_____

_____

Week 35

CREATING PERSONAL POLICIES

Everybody loves talking about boundaries—so much so that I feel like the word has morphed from an important and useful concept into a buzzword annoyingly co-opted by people who don't know what it means. Instead, I've started using the term "personal policies": things I will and won't do based on my personal values. Personal policies are way chiller-sounding, but they are just as strong as boundaries. And they don't have to be negative—they can be fun! Some of mine are to never lower my dating standards, to always have one night a week to myself, and to not be friends with people who try to make me feel insecure.

How do you want people to treat you? (Be more specific than just saying, "Kindly.") What treatment do you not want to tolerate?

_____

_____

_____

_____

_____

_____

_____

_____

_____

_____

What are some personal policies you're committed to—things
you commit to doing or *not* doing?

_____

_____

_____

_____

_____

_____

_____

_____

_____

_____

_____

What are some things that may be harming you right now that you're having trouble letting go of? What are some personal policies you could implement to make changes in these areas?

_____

_____

_____

_____

_____

_____

_____

_____

_____

_____

_____

_____

Week 36

RELYING ON OTHERS

The words "ambitious" and "independent" are often used in the same sentence to describe people—and I am one of those people. I not only want to do things myself and like to do things myself, I also know it's usually *better* when I do things myself! Except for when I can't do anything I need or want to do because I'm so overwhelmed. Or someone on my team is more skilled at this task. Or I simply don't have time in the day. The truth is, when you want to do a lot, you must rely on your community and connections for help. It can be scary, but think about how much joy and connection you get out of helping others—why can't that also be true for people helping you?

Are you afraid of getting help from others? Why or why not?

_____

_____

_____

_____

_____

_____

_____

_____

_____

_____

_____

Who in your life can you rely on to give you good advice when it comes to love and relationships? Who can you rely on for professional/career help? Who can you rely on for fun and joy?

_____

_____

_____

_____

_____

_____

_____

_____

_____

List one to three people who you love to connect with and why. Celebrate your community by reaching out and letting them know you appreciate them this week.

1. _____

_____

_____

2. _____

_____

_____

3. _____

_____

_____

Week 37

CAPACITY CONSTRAINTS

You know when you're so overwhelmed with what to do next that you freeze up and don't do anything? We might make jokes about feeling this way as if it's no big deal, but really, it's an indication that we're in over our heads. As ambitious people, we may have high capacities for stress, but that doesn't mean we're superhuman. You need to keep a close eye on when you're overwhelmed; otherwise burnout will take you out.

When was the last time you felt overwhelmed? How did you start to notice that you couldn't take it anymore? How often has that happened in the past year?

_____

_____

_____

_____

_____

_____

_____

_____

_____

_____

_____

_____

_____

_____

_____

_____

What are your nonnegotiable self-care practices each day, week, and month?

_____

_____

_____

_____

_____

_____

_____

_____

_____

_____

_____

_____

_____

Who can you reach out to when you're starting to feel burnt out?

_____

_____

_____

_____

_____

_____

Week 38

GETTING BACK ON TRACK

It's no secret that ambitious people are likely to experience burnout sooner or later. I've found myself at the end of my emotional rope countless times, and recently, I realized that it wasn't because I was "bad at self-care"—it was because I had too much on my plate to have any time or energy for self-care. It's okay; this happens. Don't beat yourself up; build yourself up. When I realize I'm tapped out, I give myself a couple of days to blob and process how much I've been overworking, then move on to rejuvenation and start revitalizing my life with new goals and ambitions.

When you've fallen off from your goals, how do you get more in touch with your emotions?

_____

_____

_____

_____

_____

_____

_____

_____

What practices and connections help you come back to you?

When you fall off, how can you forgive yourself and continue along your path?

_____

_____

_____

_____

_____

_____

_____

_____

_____

_____

_____

_____

_____

_____

Week 39

QUARTERLY RESET
Q3

You've made it all the way through Q3, working, learning, and growing the whole time. You've done such an amazing job putting in the work for yourself, and hopefully you're starting to see the benefits. Let's take one more big breath and reflect on the last quarter before we head into the home stretch.

Over the past three months, what were your significant achievements, and in what areas did you see the most growth? Pay attention to all areas of life: family, personal life, professional life, relationships, money, and friendships.

_____

_____

_____

_____

_____

_____

_____

Reflect on your self-care practices over the past quarter. How have these practices supported your physical, mental, and emotional well-being?

_____

_____

_____

_____

_____

_____

_____

_____

_____

_____

_____

_____

_____

Consider moments when you felt the most stressed or unbalanced. What triggered these feelings, and how did you respond? Identify patterns or recurring themes in your stressors.

_____

_____

_____

_____

_____

_____

_____

_____

_____

_____

_____

_____

_____

Think back to where you were when you started this quarter. What was that person struggling with, and how have you addressed it? What are you struggling with now, and how do you want to approach that in the next phase of your self-growth?

_____

_____

_____

_____

_____

_____

_____

_____

_____

_____

_____

_____

_____

Frameworks for Real Life

When I was graduating college, I made a spreadsheet plotting out how the next ten years of my life would look. I'd complete the entry-level marketing program at a big tech company, get my MBA, get married to my college boyfriend, become an executive at a large apparel brand, and have four children by the time I was thirty-five.

Then we had a global pandemic. And I hated the marketing program at the big tech company. And I accidentally became an influencer. And broke up with my boyfriend. And started my own company.

Each major change was scary in the moment, and I felt lost when each pillar of my life was destroyed. But on the other side of each of those shake-ups, I found something infinitely better than what was on my spreadsheet. I found a relationship with myself during the isolation of the pandemic, an amazing strategy role at a different big tech company, the ability to build community online from my influencer work, a sense of freedom that came with being single in my twenties, and a feeling of resilience from building my own business.

We often rush to craft a perfect vision of the "next level" without stopping to consider the myriad complications that might arise while we climb. The other side of setbacks can be sweeter than we can imagine, but that doesn't make the moments of truth we face when letting go of our dreams any less brutal. Throughout every transition, we will rub up against big feelings that we have to work through to see the beauty of self-love on our journeys.

To guide myself through these transitions, I've developed a different framework with which to view my life: I see time in metaphorical seasons, and I think in each season, we're meant to experience new and different things. Your routines won't be the same in every season, and your coping mechanisms will be different after each new experience. My time in business school, for example, was a season when I had to make trade-offs in order to experience new things—but those trade-offs were not a permanent strategy that defined how I lived my life.

I believe we are on this earth purely to go through the range of human emotions, embody new feelings, and love each other and ourselves as much as we can. Though we might enjoy hustling for accolades and designing our dream houses, that bliss is only part of the larger experience of what it means to be a human being. Much of this journal so far has focused on how to address who you are, allow yourself to dream, effectively introduce new habits, and tend to your soul. On a day-to-day basis, these are wonderful tools to help you through your life. But what happens when life starts to *life* and you face a big change?

The prompts in this quarter are here to serve as a landing place when you start to realize that you might be getting overwhelmed with another change in your life, whether it's an unexpected heartbreak, an itch to leave the job you once loved, or a constant, gnawing comparison bug that keeps you from realizing your full bliss. Remember that on the other side of whatever you're working through might be something better than you could've imagined.

Week 40

SELF-WORTH

You may have a stacked résumé or a "delusional" sense of confidence—or at least I hope you do after completing the first three quarters of this journal! But at our core, until we recognize our inherent self-worth, we stall in our growth. All humans, regardless of our accomplishments, are worthy. Picture a baby just entering this world. You would advocate for that baby because all humans are worthy of love and health, right? You were once that child, so why would you not be worthy too?

Do you feel there are actions you must take or things you have to accomplish in order to be worthy? What are they? Why do you feel they're necessary?

_____

_____

_____

_____

_____

_____

_____

_____

_____

_____

_____

_____

_____

Who are the biggest influences on your sense of self-worth, good or bad? What cultural factors may be affecting these influences' opinions about your self-worth?

_____

_____

_____

_____

_____

_____

_____

_____

_____

_____

_____

What would your relationship with yourself look like if you
genuinely believed you were worthy of everything you wanted?

_____

_____

_____

_____

_____

_____

_____

_____

_____

_____

_____

Week 41

MAKING BIG DECISIONS

Are you getting the inkling that it's time to move, leave a job, end a friendship, or even (gasp!) cut your hair? While change is the only constant in this life, it can be overwhelming when you're making a big life decision for yourself. It's important, especially when ending a relationship or leaving a job that may have a negative effect on you, to use data to make decisions, not just emotions (though those can be a valuable part of the process too). Here are some questions I ask myself when I get the itch to change:

When you reflect on the past few weeks or months that you were engaging with this relationship, job, or other part of your life, what are the prominent feelings that come to mind? How many times did you feel like it was giving you energy rather than taking it, and vice versa?

_____

_____

_____

_____

_____

_____

_____

_____

_____

_____

_____

_____

_____

_____

_____

_____

_____

What would be the worst-case scenario if you make this decision and it backfires? What would be the best-case scenario if you stay in this situation? Which one do you think would be worse for you?

_____

_____

_____

_____

_____

_____

_____

_____

_____

_____

_____

Look back at the values and dreams that you wrote about in Weeks 17 through 22 of this journal. Do these still align with your values and what you want for yourself?

_____

_____

_____

_____

_____

_____

Week 42

SELF-SABOTAGE

Sneaky, isn't it? That feeling when you suddenly lose all motivation to continue a project you were obsessed with the week before. Or the day you pick that fight with the only person who's given you butterflies in years. Things were going well—so well, in fact, that you started to get scared of what changes might start to happen, and you did something stupid to make sure you stayed in your comfort zone. Self-sabotage is harmful, but we can also see it as a wonderful messenger of when we're hitting a ceiling in our growth because it's a subconscious reaction to positive change. And we have control over our actions, so we can stop this sabotage in its tracks when we notice it.

What are some self-sabotaging behaviors that you engage in? What are the signs that you're starting to self-sabotage, and how has this affected you in the past? Can you forgive yourself for this?

_____

_____

_____

_____

_____

_____

_____

_____

_____

_____

_____

_____

_____

_____

_____

_____

_____

What are you afraid might happen if you move forward in this situation? What feelings might this self-sabotage be protecting you from?

_____

_____

_____

_____

_____

_____

_____

_____

_____

_____

_____

When you start to notice self-sabotaging behaviors, who can you reach out to to hold yourself accountable? How can you remind yourself to stop this behavior before it creates problems for you?

_____

_____

_____

_____

_____

Week 43

FEELING STUCK

When life starts to feel blah, or the next step isn't so clear, it's time to reconnect with yourself and make a change. Feeling stuck is the best indication that your soul is ready for more, so it's a perfect time to start daydreaming again or go back to cherished activities that always inspire you or make you feel alive.

If you're feeling stuck, when did it start? When was the last time in your life that you felt excited and motivated? How can you cultivate that again?

_____

_____

_____

_____

_____

_____

_____

_____

_____

_____

_____

_____

_____

_____

_____

When you look at the future you dreamed up for yourself, does it still align with what you want now? What's the next thing you can do to get there?

_____

_____

_____

_____

_____

_____

We often feel stuck because we're doing the same thing too often. What are one to three changes you can make in your routine this week to experience something new?

_____

_____

_____

_____

_____

_____

_____

_____

_____

_____

_____

_____

_____

Week 44

CONSISTENCY AND SELF-DISCIPLINE

Consistency and self-discipline are two factors that are constantly praised in the self-improvement space, and there are tons of habit-building tips out there. But the real trick is that it all comes back to self-worth. When we believe that we're inherently worthy of the things we want, we don't struggle as much with consistency and self-discipline. The quote "Treat yourself like your child" helps me embody this. If I had a daughter, I wouldn't want her to have so much fear and shame about her body that she didn't take care of herself. I'd tell her she was amazing and give her the right structure so that consistency would be easy for her. Can you do that for yourself?

In what area do you struggle the most with consistency?
What might this reveal about how worthy you feel of having control over that area of your life?

_____

_____

_____

_____

_____

_____

_____

_____

_____

_____

_____

_____

_____

_____

_____

_____

Where have you been successfully able to introduce a habit and stick to it? Why was that particular habit possible for you?

_____

_____

_____

_____

_____

_____

_____

_____

_____

_____

If you were treating yourself like your child, how could you create more ease around consistency so that you were able to be consistent more easily?

_____

_____

_____

_____

_____

_____

_____

Week 45

HOW TO BE MORE CONFIDENT

In my experience, there are three ways to increase your confidence, and they are all different. You can anxiously accumulate accolades (been there, lol), you can try to fake it till you make it (throwback to when I acted like Blair Waldorf all of freshman year of high school because I thought that was true "confidence"), or you can actually build your self-trust by nourishing yourself. The last one is the only one that really works in a deep and lasting way. It takes time, but luckily, you're already on your way!

What are some fundamental aspects of your personality that you may have hidden from others or may not be confident in? What would it look like if you embraced these things instead of trying to change them?

_____

_____

_____

_____

_____

_____

_____

_____

_____

_____

When you visualize confidence, who do you see? This could be a
celebrity, a fictional character, someone you work with—anyone
who embodies confidence. What does this person do or say that
you can emulate to build your own confidence?

_____

_____

_____

_____

_____

_____

_____

_____

_____

What are some reasons that you have to be proud of yourself? (Hint: taking the time to journal and learn about yourself is one of them!)

_____

_____

_____

_____

_____

_____

_____

_____

_____

_____

_____

_____

Week 46

HANDLING FAILURE

Little hurts more than realizing that you have, in fact, failed at something. Maybe at work, maybe at home, or maybe with yourself. But as time goes on, you will start to realize that failure is simply a lesson on how to do better in the future, proof that you tried, and an opportunity to rise up. When you fail, it is in your best interest to admit it, learn from it, and move on. Failure is a gift!

Think about a specific recent failure—it could be big or small. Keeping your values in mind, write out the things that led to your failure. Were you acting in alignment with your values? How can you acknowledge and remedy this mistake? How can you avoid it in the future?

_____

_____

_____

_____

_____

_____

_____

_____

_____

_____

_____

_____

_____

_____

_____

_____

What's the best lesson you can take with you moving forward? How might you be able to help other people now that you've failed in this area?

_____

_____

_____

_____

_____

_____

_____

_____

_____

_____

_____

_____

If failure is really stinging, take a second to Google people in your field who have failed and come back from it. This could even be Googling one of your biggest inspirations and reading more about their story. (A particularly impactful one for me was Issa Rae. I had never known that she'd failed at developing a show with fellow TV icon Shonda Rhimes before creating the award-winning *Insecure* series later on.) Whose story resonates, and how can you remind yourself of this when you're feeling low?

_____

_____

_____

_____

_____

_____

Week 47

HANDLING HEARTBREAK

"Soul crushing" is the best way to describe how it felt to end a six-year relationship with someone I thought I was going to marry. The failed situationships in the months thereafter were uniquely soul emptying too. Most of us have had our hearts broken, usually more than once. But once we get over the ego crush and the emotional whiplash, it's fun to remember that we *get to fall in love again* one day. Isn't that special?

Think about your ideal partner or what you believe a healthy relationship looks like, which you wrote about in Week 6 of this journal. Did the person who broke your heart match these ideals, or were they just there? Where were you settling or not showing up as your best self?

_____

_____

_____

_____

_____

_____

_____

_____

_____

_____

_____

_____

_____

_____

List three data-driven reasons why this person wasn't right for you. (If you're struggling here, remember, someone not being excited about you is reason number one they aren't for you!)

_____

_____

_____

_____

_____

_____

_____

_____

_____

_____

_____

Think about the love you deserve in life. How can you give that to yourself while you ache right now?

_____

_____

_____

_____

_____

_____

_____

_____

_____

Week 48

RELEASING GUILT

As the eldest daughter, when I left my seven younger siblings in my hometown to go to college, my big-sister guilt manifested in feeling the need to control their lives. It wasn't until after I'd graduated that I recognized this guilt was holding me back from living my own life, and that the shame I felt was not based in reality. When we're driven by guilt or shame, especially in a situation where we haven't actually done anything wrong, we only create more turmoil for ourselves and others. Releasing it is the only way forward.

What are you feeling guilty about? Is this situation truly your emotional responsibility to carry? If not, why does it feel that way?

_____

_____

_____

_____

_____

_____

_____

_____

_____

_____

_____

_____

_____

_____

If the situation is interpersonal, you are at fault to some degree, and you can and have apologized, what keeps you focused on it? What might you be afraid this reveals about you?

_____

_____

_____

_____

_____

_____

_____

_____

_____

_____

How can you learn from this guilt and transform it into a mantra about taking care of yourself? What would that mantra be?

_____

_____

_____

_____

_____

_____

_____

_____

_____

_____

Week 49

THE COMPARISON TRAP

How much time do you think we've wasted comparing our bodies, accomplishments, résumés, facial structure, nail beds, style, and every other little thing about ourselves to others? It all seems foolish when you realize that in order for you to have the exact same outcomes as someone else, you would have to have the exact same experiences, upbringing, resources, and so on. It's basic math. We're all different, and our dreams are all different, so comparing yourself to someone else is like trying to compare the beauty of a flower grown in a greenhouse to the beauty of one grown on a craggy seaside cliff.

Where do you struggle the most with comparing yourself to others? What standard are you holding yourself to, and what do you think it means about you if you do or don't reach it?

_____

_____

_____

_____

_____

_____

_____

_____

_____

_____

_____

_____

_____

_____

Think of the person who is triggering your urge to compare the
most. Look at your backgrounds and note how different they
are. Can you identify why you might have different outcomes,
and then create a version of success for yourself based on your
situation alone?

_____

_____

_____

_____

_____

_____

_____

_____

_____

_____

_____

_____

How can you transform your envy toward this person into motivation?

_____

_____

_____

_____

_____

_____

_____

Week 50

SAYING NO

It's my belief that people-pleasing creates more resentment in this world than deliberate rudeness. People-pleasing isn't just being nice; it's catering to others even when it's bad for you or out of alignment with your needs or values. When we say yes to things that aren't aligned with our goals and ideals, we only delay ourselves from doing what we're really meant to do. In truth, the temporary pain of "disappointing" someone by not catering to them is worth the long-term alignment with what we desire.

What are you afraid will happen when you say no or set a boundary with someone? Why are you afraid of that?

_____

_____

_____

_____

_____

_____

_____

_____

_____

_____

Identify an area of your life where you've been able to set great
boundaries. Now think about the area of your life where you
have the hardest time saying no. What makes these two things
different, and how can you integrate good boundaries into the
area where that's more challenging?

_____

_____

_____

_____

_____

_____

_____

_____

_____

Write out your priorities for this phase in your life, and practice referring to them when you're asked to do something that isn't part of your plan. How does this influence your response to that ask?

_____

_____

_____

_____

_____

_____

_____

_____

_____

_____

_____

_____

Week 51

ACCEPTING LOVE

When we've been on guard for our entire lives, it can feel scary to accept success and love into our lives. But the essence of human connection is love, and we miss out on the most beautiful, blissful parts of life when we don't allow ourselves to feel the full sense of it all.

In what areas of your life have you been hiding because you're afraid of being your full self? How do you think your behavior would change if you released that shame and acted more authentically?

_____

_____

_____

_____

_____

_____

_____

_____

Who can you practice being your full self around? What about them makes you feel safe?

_____

_____

_____

_____

_____

_____

_____

_____

Think about someone who has shown love to you recently, whether through actions or words. Were you able to accept that love, or did you shut it out? Why do you think that is?

_____

_____

_____

_____

_____

_____

_____

_____

_____

_____

How does love feel to you? How can you give that to yourself?

_____

_____

_____

_____

_____

_____

_____

_____

_____

Week 52

QUARTERLY RESET
Q4

Wow! You've made it to the end of this journal. What an accomplishment: you stood up to do the work on yourself, and now you're on the other side of it. Now take some time to be even prouder of yourself by looking back on what you've learned and how you've grown.

Over the past year, what were your significant achievements, and in what areas did you see the most growth? Pay attention to the areas of life we touched on: family, personal life, professional life, relationships, money, and friendships.

_____

_____

_____

_____

_____

_____

_____

_____

Reflect on your self-care practices over the past year. How have these practices supported your physical, mental, and emotional well-being? How have they changed in different life seasons and as you learned more and more about yourself?

_____

_____

_____

_____

_____

_____

_____

_____

_____

_____

_____

_____

_____

_____

Consider moments when you felt the most stressed or unbalanced.
What triggered these feelings, and how did you respond? Identify
patterns or recurring themes in your stressors. How would
the person who started this journal react to these moments as
opposed to the person you are today?

_____

_____

_____

_____

_____

_____

_____

_____

_____

_____

_____

_____

Name at least five things you're proud of yourself for doing this past year. (Completing this journal can definitely be one of them!) How has connecting with yourself helped you feel stronger?

_____

_____

_____

_____

_____

_____

_____

_____

_____

_____

_____

_____

About the Author

ALEXIS BARBER is a digital creator and the founder of Too Collective, a leisure company that makes it easy to incorporate self-care into your daily life. Her podcast, *Too Smart for This*, which features wellness-focused interviews with female entrepreneurs, was ranked the best motivational podcast by *Cosmopolitan* in 2021. Previously a global content strategist at YouTube, she holds an MBA from the Wharton School at the University of Pennsylvania.